SRZ TRADING STRATEGY

UNLOCKING FINANCIAL FREEDOM

M. KAI ZOLLINGER

CONTENTS

Stock Market Introduction

What is the Stock Market?

Think of the stock market as a vast marketplace where institutions and individuals buy and sell company ownership shares. It's where businesses raise money by issuing shares to the public through initial public offerings (IPOs), and investors go to potentially grow their wealth. Imagine it as a place where you canbuy and trade pieces of companies, and the value of those pieces goes up and down based on how well those companies are doing and what people are willingto pay for them. It's a hub of financial activity where millions of people and institutions come together to invest, speculate, and participate in the global economy.

Types of Stock Markets:

1.   *Primary Market:* The primary stock market is where companies first introduce their shares to the public through IPOs. During an IPO, companies sellsome of their ownership (shares) to investors in exchange for capital. This market is where the first transactions of the newly issued shares occur. After theIPO, these shares can then be traded in the secondary market by individual and institutional investors.

2.   *Secondary Market:* The secondary market trades previously issued stocksby individual and institutional investors. Unlike the primary market, where companies raise capital by

issuing new shares, the secondary market is where investors trade these existing shares with one another. It's like a continuous exchange where people buy and sell stocks based on their perceived value. Stock exchanges, like the New York Stock Exchange (NYSE) and the NASDAQ, are examples of venues where these transactions take place.

3.   *Over-the-Counter (OTC) Market:* The OTC market is a less formalized but critically important segment of the financial world, functioning as a decentralizedmarketplace where various financial instruments, including stocks, bonds, currencies, and derivatives, are traded directly between buyers and sellers. Unlike highly organized and regulated exchanges like the New York Stock Exchange or the NASDAQ, the OTC market operates more fluidly and flexibly, serving as a pivotal nexus for a wide range of assets.

Key Components:

1.   *Investors:* The stock market is home to a diverse range of participants, including individual retail investors, day traders, institutional investors, mutualfunds, pension funds, hedge funds, and even governments. Each group brings its objectives, strategies, and time horizons to the market.

2.   *Traders:* Traders seek short-term profits by buying and selling stocks quickly. They may use various strategies, including scalping, day trading, andswing trading.

3. ***Brokers and Exchanges:*** Stock exchanges are the primary venues where stocks are bought and sold. Major exchanges, like the New York Stock Exchange and NASDAQ, provide the infrastructure for trading and set the stagefor daily market activities.

4. ***Regulatory Oversight:*** Regulatory bodies, such as the Securities and Exchange Commission (SEC) in the United States, play a critical role in overseeing the stock market ensuring fair practices, transparency, and investorprotection.

5. ***Stocks:*** Stocks, also known as equities or shares, represent ownership in acompany. When individuals or institutions hold stocks, they have a stake in the company's assets, earnings, and, to some extent, decision-making.

6. ***Market Indices:*** Market indices, like the S&P 500, Dow Jones Industrial Average, or NASDAQ Composite, provide snapshots of how a particular market segment is performing. These indices track the collective performance of a select group of stocks, often representing specific industries or market sectors.

Market Participants:

1. ***Retail Investors:*** These are individual investors who buy and sell stocks through brokerage accounts. They include everyone from first-time investors toseasoned traders.

2.   *Institutional investors:* This group includes hedge funds, mutual funds, pension funds, and insurance companies. They manage large pools of capital and play a significant role in the market.

3.   *Traders:* Traders are individuals or institutions who frequently buy and sell stocks, often on a short-term basis. They aim to profit from price fluctuations.

Market Mechanisms:

1.   *Bull and Bear Markets:* The stock market experiences periods of upwardand downward trends. Rising stock prices characterize a bull market, while a bear market sees falling prices.

2.   *Technical and Fundamental Analysis:* Investors use various tools and strategies to analyze stocks. Technical analysis relies on historical price and volume data, while fundamental analysis assesses a company's financial healthand growth prospects.

3.   *Trading Strategies:* Investors employ diverse trading strategies, such as day trading, value investing, growth investing, and dividend investing, to achievetheir financial goals.

Significance of the Stock Market:

The stock market is a multifaceted ecosystem that reflects the ever-changing dynamics of the global economy. Its functions, participants, and mechanisms make it a crucial component of modern finance, shaping individuals, corporations, and nations' financial well-being. Understanding its intricacies andstaying informed about market developments is essential for anyone seeking to navigate the complex world of investments.

Trading Styles

Scalp Trading:

Scalp trading, often called "scalping," is a short-term trading strategy traders use in various financial markets, including stocks, forex, commodities, and cryptocurrencies. The primary objective of scalp trading is to profit from smallprice movements over short timeframes, ranging from seconds to minutes.

Scalpers execute numerous trades throughout the trading session with the goalof accumulating small gains that, when combined, will result in a profitable outcome.

Elements of Scalp Trading:

1.   *Short Holding Period:* Scalpers typically hold positions briefly, often just a few seconds to a few minutes. They do not usually hold positions overnight, asthe focus is on capitalizing on intraday price fluctuations.

2.   *Intraday Focus:* Scalping is exclusively an intraday strategy, meaning alltrades are open and closed within the same trading session. This approach avoids overnight risks associated with price gaps caused by news events or market sentiment shifts.

3.   *Small Price Targets:* Scalpers set small profit targets for each trade, oftenjust a few cents or pips. These targets are designed to capture the immediate price movement and lock in

profits quickly.

4.   *High-Frequency Trading:* Scalpers execute many trades during a singletrading session, sometimes numbering in the dozens or hundreds.

5.   *Technical Analysis:* Scalpers use technical analysis to identify possible entry and exit points. They use a variety of indicators, chart patterns, and real-time market data to make quick decisions.

6.   *Risk Management:* Given the rapid pace of scalping, traders implement strict risk management. Proper risk management is used by setting tight stop-loss orders to limit potential losses.

7.   *Liquidity:* Scalp traders will likely prefer highly liquid markets with a tight bid-ask spread. In these markets, with a small spread, there is less slippage (thedifference between the expected and the executed price), which is ideal for capturing small price movements.

8.   *Level II Data:* Scalpers often use Level II quotes and market depth data to gauge real-time supply and demand dynamics.

9.   *Profitability from Volume:* Scalping relies on taking advantage of the cumulative impact of many small price movements. While each trade may yielda small profit, the incremental gains can be significant.

10.   **Speed and Precision:** Scalpers must be quick and decisive when enteringor exiting a trade. The goal is to capture small price fluctuations quickly.

11.   *Discipline:* Scalping can be mentally demanding due to the need for rapid decision-making and handling multiple trades. Maintaining discipline, sticking to atrading plan, and avoiding emotional reactions are crucial for success.

12.   *Transactions Costs:* Scalping can result in substantial transaction costs, such as spreads and commissions, which must be considered when evaluatingthe strategy's profitability.

Note: Scalp trading is not for all traders, as it requires a unique skill set, tolerance for high-stress levels, and the ability to make quick decisions in a fast-paced environment. Additionally, the cost associated with scalp trading can consume profits if not managed correctly - experienced traders who have developed specific strategies and risk management techniques, primarily scalp trade.

Intraday Trading:

Intraday trading, also known as day trading, is a trading strategy in which traders buy and sell financial assets within the same day. Unlike traditional investing, where investors may hold positions for days, weeks, months, or evenyears, intraday traders seek to profit from short-term price movements over a much shorter timeframe, often within minutes or hours.

Elements of Intraday Trading:

1.   ***Short-Term Focus:*** Intraday traders aim to capitalize on price fluctuationsduring the trading day and avoid overnight market risks. All positions are typically closed by the end of the trading session.

2.   ***Frequent Trading:*** Day traders execute multiple trades within a single trading day, taking advantage of various short-term opportunities in the market.

3.   ***Technical Analysis:*** Intraday trading often relies on technical analysis, usingtools such as charts, indicators, and patterns to identify potential entry and exit points.

4.   ***Margin Trading:*** Some intraday traders use margin accounts, allowing themto borrow funds to trade more significant positions. This leverage can amplify both gains and losses.

5.   ***Risk Management:*** Effective risk management is crucial in day-trading.Traders often use stop-loss orders to limit potential losses on each trade.

6.   ***Liquidity Volatility:*** Intraday traders prefer markets with high liquidity and volatility, as these conditions provide opportunities for price movements that can beexploited for profit.

7.   ***Time Commitment:*** Day trading requires a significant time commitment, astraders must actively monitor the markets, make quick decisions, and execute trades throughout the trading day.

8. ***Discipline:*** The fast-paced nature of day-trading can be emotionally demanding. Traders must maintain discipline, adhere to their trading plans, andavoid making impulsive decisions based on emotions.

9. ***Regulatory Considerations:*** Some regulatory bodies may impose specific rules and requirements on day trading, including minimum capital requirementsand restrictions on pattern day trading.

10. ***Transactions Costs:*** Frequent trading can result in substantial transactioncosts, including spreads, commissions, and fees. Traders need to account for these costs when evaluating the profitability of their trades.

Note: It's important to note that intraday trading is not suitable for all individuals, and it carries a high level of risk. While it offers the potential for quick profits, it alsoinvolves the risk of significant losses, especially when leverage is used. Successful day trading requires a deep understanding of the chosen market, technical analysisskills, effective risk management, and the ability to stay disciplined in a fast-paced environment. It is a trading style commonly pursued by experienced and knowledgeable traders who are well-prepared for their demands.

Swing Trading

Swing trading is a strategy used in financial markets where traders aim to profit from price "swings" or short to medium-term price movements in an asset. Unlikeday trading, which involves buying and selling within the same trading day, swing trading typically involves holding positions for several days to weeks to capture price moves during that time frame.

Elements of Swing Trading:

1.   *Time Horizon:* Swing traders have a longer time horizon than day traders. They hold positions for days, weeks, or sometimes even months, depending on the specific trading strategy and market conditions.

2.   *Technical Analysis:* Swing traders rely heavily on technical analysis, using tools such as charts, indicators, and patterns to identify potential entry and exit points. Common technical indicators for swing trading include moving averages, the Relative Strength Index (RSI), and the MACD (Moving Average Convergence Divergence).

3.   *Price Swings:* Swing traders seek to profit from price swings within a trend. They aim to enter positions when they anticipate a price reversal or continuation of the existing trend.

4.   *Risk Management:* Effective risk management is essential in swing trading. Traders use stop-loss orders to limit potential losses and set profit targets to lock in gains. By doing this, it helps maintain a favorable risk-reward ratio.

5.   *Fundamental Analysis:* Some swing traders may incorporate fundamental analysis into their trading decisions, especially when trading stocks. They may consider factors like

earnings reports, company news, and economic data.

6. **_Market Liquidity:_** Swing traders typically prefer assets with sufficient liquidity, ensuring they can enter and exit positions without significant slippage(the difference between the expected price and the execution price).

7. **_Diversification:_** Swing traders often maintain a diversified portfolio of positions to spread risk. Diversification can help mitigate the impact of poorperformance on a single asset.

8. **_Time Commitment:_** Swing trading requires a moderate time commitment compared to day trading. Traders must monitor their positions periodically and adjust their strategies based on changing market conditions.

9. **Discipline:** While not as fast-paced as scalping or intraday trading, swing trading still requires discipline. Traders must stick to their trading plans, manageemotions, and avoid impulsive decisions.

10. **Regulatory Considerations:** Depending on your location and the assets you trade, there may be regulatory requirements and tax implications associatedwith swing trading.

Note: Swing trading can balance the shorter timeframes of day trading and the longer-term horizons of traditional investing. It allows traders to capture intermediate price movements while avoiding the stress of constant monitoringassociated with day trading. Successful swing trading involves a combination of technical and, in some cases, fundamental analysis, along with prudent risk management.

Trading One vs. Multiple Stocks

Trade One or Multiple Stocks?

Trading one stock instead of several, also known as focusing on a single stockor having a concentrated trading approach, can have advantages and

disadvantages. Trading one or multiple stocks depends on your trading strategy,risk tolerance, and investment goals. Here are some reasons to focus on one stock.

Advantages of Trading One Stock:

1.   *Specialization:* Trading a single stock allows you to become highly specialized and knowledgeable about that specific company and its stock pricebehavior. This in-depth knowledge can provide a competitive edge.

2.   *Focused Research:* You can dedicate more time to researching and analyzing one stock, enabling you to make more informed decisions based onfundamental and technical analysis.

3.   *Reduced Complexity:* Managing multiple stock positions can be complexand time-consuming. Trading one stock simplifies the process and may lead tobetter decision-making.

4.   *Emotional Control:* Concentrating on one stock may help you maintainbetter emotional control. You can avoid feeling overwhelmed or making impulsive decisions with fewer

monitoring positions.

5.   *Capital Allocation:* By concentrating your capital on one stock, you can allocate more resources to that trade, which may lead to more significant profitsif the trade succeeds.

Disadvantages of Trading One Stock:

1.   *Diversification Risk:* Trading only one stock exposes you to company-specific risks. If the stock experiences a significant adverse event or price decline, it can substantially impact your trading account.

2.   *Limited Opportunities:* Relying on a single stock, limits your trading opportunities. You may miss out on other potentially profitable trades when thatstock is not exhibiting favorable trading conditions.

3.   *High Risk:* With concentrated positions, the risk is concentrated as well. Ifthe stock experiences unexpected adverse movements, it can result in more significant losses.

4.   Market Dependency: Your trading success becomes highly dependent on the performance of a single stock, which may only sometimes align with broadermarket trends.

5.   *Lack of Diversification:* A concentrated approach, a common risk management strategy, can lack diversification. Diversifying across multipleassets can help spread the risk.

Note: Trading one stock or several depends on your trading goals and risk tolerance. Some traders succeed in specializing and concentrating their efforts on a single stock, while others prefer diversification and trading multiple assets to spread risk. It's essential to carefully consider your trading strategy, conduct thorough research, and manage risk effectively, regardless of whether you focuson one stock or trade multiple stocks.

Support and Resistance

In the context of stock trading and technical analysis, "support" and "resistance" are two critical concepts that describe price levels at which a stock tends to stop orreverse its trend. Traders and analysts use these levels to make informed trading decisions and identify potential entry and exit points.

Support:

· **Definition:** Support is a price level at which a stock or market tends to findbuying interest, preventing it from falling further. It is like a "floor" for the price, where demand for the stock increases, and selling pressure decreases, causing the stock price to bounce back or consolidate.

· **Significance:** Support levels are essential because they indicate areas where traders believe the stock could be seen as undervalued, making it an attractive buy opportunity. When the stock price approaches a known supportlevel, some traders may enter long positions (buy), expecting the price to rebound.

· **Role:** Support levels can be used by traders and investors to set profit- taking targets or to monitor the stock's behavior. A break below a support level can be a bearish signal, suggesting the potential for further price decline.

Resistance:

· **Definition:** Resistance is a level at which a stock tends to encounter selling interest, preventing it from rising further. It acts as a "ceiling" for the price, where the supply of the stock increases, and buying interest decreases, causing the stockprice to stall or reverse.

·   *Significance:* Resistance levels are significant because they represent pricepoints where traders believe the stock is overvalued or may face external pressures. Some traders may consider selling or taking profits when the stock price approaches a known resistance level.

·   *Role:* Resistance levels can be used by traders and investors to set profit-taking targets or to monitor the stock's behavior. A break above a resistance

level can be a bullish signal, suggesting the potential for further price appreciation.

Note: Traders and technical analysts often use various tools and indicators to identify support and resistance levels, such as trend lines, moving averages, Fibonacci retracement, and pivot points. These levels are not fixed and can change over time as market dynamics evolve. Strong support or resistance levels are typically associated with round numbers or psychologically significantprice levels.

Understanding support and resistance levels can be valuable in formulating tradingstrategies, managing risk, and making informed decisions in the stock market.

However, it's essential to note that no price level works with absolute certainty, andtechnical analysis should be used in conjunction with other forms of analysis and risk management techniques when making trading decisions.

Candlesticks

Bullish and Bearish Candles:

In technical analysis (TA), "bullish" and "bearish" candles refer to specific candlestick patterns that provide insights into the price behavior of a stock or assetover a particular period. Candlestick patterns help assess the market's sentiment, assisting traders in making decisions.

Bullish Candle:

A bullish candlestick is a candle whose closing price is higher than its opening price, indicating that the price of the stock or asset increased during the specified period. Bullish candles are associated with positive market sentimentand potential buying pressure. Characteristics of a bullish candle include:

·   *Opening Price (Open):* The price at which the candle opens, typicallyrepresented by the bottom of the candle's body.

·   *Closing Price (Close):* The price at which the candle closes, typicallyrepresented by the top of the candle's body.

·   *Upper Shadow/Wick:* The thin line extending above the candle's body,indicating the highest price reached during the period.

·   *Lower Shadow/Wick:* The thin line extending below the candle's bodyindicates the lowest price reached during the period.

Note: A bullish candlestick suggests that buyers dominated during the specifiedperiod and that the price trend may continue upward or experience a bullish reversal.

Bearish Candle:

A bearish candlestick is a candle whose closing price is lower than its opening price, indicating that the price of the stock or asset decreased during the specified period. Bearish candles are associated with negative market sentimentand potential selling pressure. Characteristics of a bearish candle include:

·   *Opening Price (Open):* The price at which the candle opens, typicallyrepresented by the top of the candle's body.

·   *Closing Price (Close):* The price at which the candle closes, typicallyrepresented by the bottom of the candle's body.

·   *Upper Shadow/Wick:* The thin line extending above the candle's body,indicating the highest price reached during the period.

·   *Lower Shadow/Wick:* The thin line extending below the candle's bodyindicates the lowest price reached during the period.

Note: A bearish candlestick suggests that sellers dominated during the specifiedperiod and that the price trend may continue downward or experience a bearish reversal. Traders often analyze patterns of bullish and bearish candles in combination with other indicators and chart patterns to make trading decisions.

These candlestick patterns are valuable for assessing market sentiment and potential price reversals. Still, traders should use these with other forms of technical analysis and proper risk management strategies. In the diagram belowshows the difference between a bullish and bearish candle.

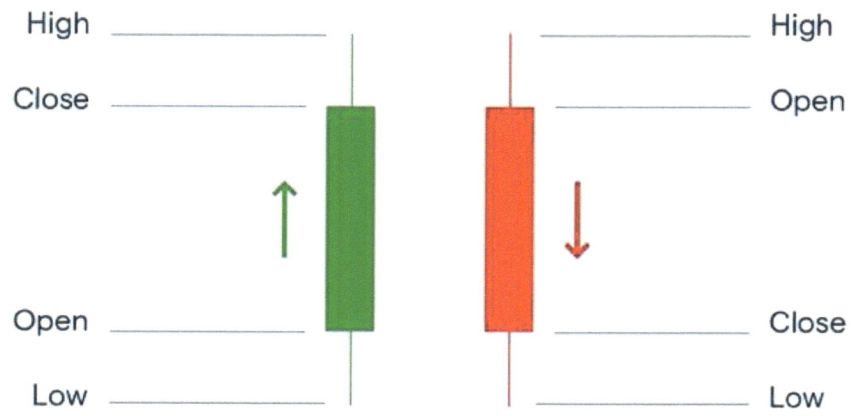

Moving Averages

Moving Averages (MA):

Definition: A moving average is a calculated average of a stock's price over a specific period, continuously updated as new data becomes available. It reduces noise and emphasizes the underlying trend in the stock's price movement.

Characteristics and Types of Moving Averages:

1.   ***Periods:*** Moving averages can be calculated over various periods, from short-term to long-term. Common periods include 50-day, 100-day, and 200-day moving averages.

2.   ***Simple Moving Average (SMA):*** The SMA is one of stock analysis's most commonly used moving averages. It provides a straightforward calculation of the average price over specific periods. Popular SMA time frames include the 50-day and 200-day moving averages. The 50-day SMA is often used for short-

term trends, while the 200-SMA is used for longer-term trends and is considereda key indicator for assessing the overall health of a stock.

3.   ***Exponential Moving Average (EMA):*** The exponential moving average gives more weight to recent prices, making it more responsive to recent pricechanges.

How Moving Averages Are Used:

·   *Trend Identification:* Moving averages help traders and investors identify trends in stock prices. When the stock's price is above the moving average, it may indicate an uptrend, while a price below the moving average may suggest adowntrend.

·   *Support and Resistance:* Moving averages may act as support and resistance levels. For example, if a stock's price approaches a rising movingaverage, it may find support. Conversely, it may encounter resistance if it approaches a falling moving average.

·   *Crossovers:* A moving average crossover is a crucial technical analysis concept used in stock trading. It occurs when two moving averages of a stock'sprice cross each other on a price chart. Typically, these moving averages have different timeframes, and their crossovers can provide necessary signals aboutthe stock trend. A bullish crossover is when a shorter-term moving average crosses above a longer-term moving average, known as a golden cross. A bearish crossover is when a shorter-term moving average crosses below a longer-term moving average, known as a death cross.

·   *Volatility Assessment:* Moving averages can also provide insights into thevolatility of a stock. Wider gaps between short-term and long-term moving averages may indicate higher volatility, while narrow gaps may suggest lower volatility.

· **_Trading Strategies:_** Traders often use moving averages to develop tradingstrategies, such as trend-following or trend-reversal strategies. For example, atrader might buy when the stock's price crosses above a moving average and sell when it crosses below.

Note: Moving averages are a versatile tool in stock analysis. Traders often usemoving averages alongside other technical indicators and chart patterns whenmaking trading decisions. The choice of which moving average to use, and thespecific trading strategy will depend on an individual's trading style, whether scalping, intraday trading or swing trading.

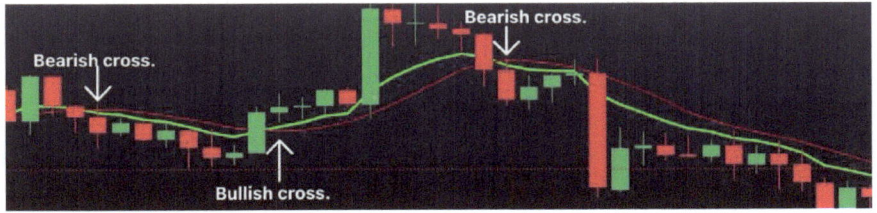

Dynamic Flow Indicator

The Dynamic Flow Indicator is an all-in-one comprehensive market analysis tool that combines the power of momentum, money flow, RSI (Relative Strength Index), VWAP (Volume-Weighted Average Price), and the Squeeze Indicator to provide traders with valuable insights into market trends.

Elements of the Flow Indicator:

1.   *Momentum:* The momentum component of this indicator tracks the speedat which stock prices change over a specific period. It helps identify the strengthof prevailing trends and potential shifts in momentum. By analyzing the rate of price changes, traders can spot potential breakout or reversal points.

2.   *Money Flow:* The money flow aspect of the indicator evaluates the volumeof money flowing into or out of a particular asset. It combines both price and volume data to gauge the strength of buyer and seller activity. Positive money flow signals increasing buying pressure, while negative money flow indicates increasing selling pressure.

3.   *RSI (Relative Strength Index):* The RSI in stock trading is like a speedometer for the stock price movements. It measures how fast and stronglythe price of a stock changes, helping traders determine if a stock might be getting overbought (too expensive) or oversold (too cheap). When the RSI is toohigh, it suggests the stock might be due for a retracement, and when it's

low, it could indicate a potential upward move.

4. ***RSI Bullish and Bearish Signals:*** When the RSI crosses above 70, it is a bearish signal, suggesting that the asset may be overbought and due for a pullback. When the RSI crosses below 30, it is a bullish signal, suggesting thatthe asset may be oversold and due for a bounce.

5. ***RSI Divergence:*** RSI divergence in stock trading is a powerful concept that helps traders identify potential reversals or shifts in a stock's price trend. Imagine itas a kind of disagreement between two friends: the Relative Strength Index (RSI) and the stock's actual price movement.

Bullish Divergence: This occurs when the RSI makes higher lows while the stock'sprice makes lower lows. It's like one friend (the RSI) is saying, "Hey, things are looking up," while the other friend (the stock price) is saying, "Not so fast, I'm still going down."

The divergence between the two suggests that the stock's downward momentummight weaken, and a price reversal to the upside could be on the horizon.

Bearish Divergence: On the flip side, bearish divergence happens when the RSI makes lower highs while the stock's price makes higher highs. It's as if one

friend (the RSI) is cautioning, "This upward trend is losing steam," while the other friend (the stock price) is saying, "I'm still climbing." The divergence would suggestthat the stock prices' upward momentum might be fading, and a potential reversalto the downside could be looming.

Note: In both cases, RSI divergence is like a warning sign that the stock's price trend might be losing strength or about to change direction. Traders use this divergence as a valuable tool to make more informed decisions about when to buyor sell stocks.

5.   *VWPA (Volume-Weighted Average Price):* VWAP calculates the average price of a stock based on both volume and price data throughout the trading day. This indicator is particularly valuable for intraday trading as it helps identifythe fair price level based on the most recent trading activity.

6.   *Squeeze Indicator:* The squeeze indicator is like a pressure gauge for pricemovements. It's a tool used in technical analysis to identify moments when a stock's price experiences lower volatility like a spring being compressed. Duringthese "squeeze" periods, the stock's price trades within a narrow range. Traders watch for these squeeze situations because they often precede significant price breakouts or breakdowns. When the pressure is released, the stock's price can suddenly and substantially move upward or downward. The squeeze indicator doesn't predict the direction of the move, but it alerts tradersto prepare for a potentially significant price shift. In essence, the squeeze indicator helps traders spot moments of calm before the

storm's potential in stock price moves, enabling them to plan their trading strategies accordingly.

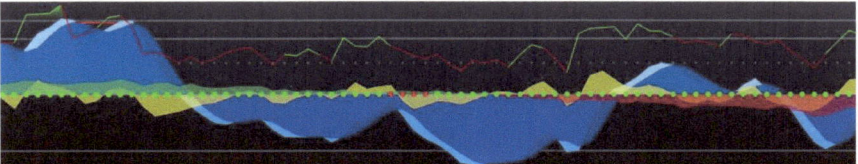

Option Chain

An option chain is a critical tool in the world of financial markets, offering a comprehensive and detailed snapshot of available options contracts associatedwith a specific underlying asset, such as a stock, exchange-traded fund (EFT), or index. This intricate mosaic of data provides traders and investors with a structured view of options contracts, complete with varying strike prices, expiration dates, and types (calls and puts) for the chosen asset.

Stock options, often seen as the financial instruments for savvy traders and investors, come up unique terminology. Among the key terms, "at the money," and"out of the money" hold pivotal significance. These designations, though concise, encapsulate critical aspects of options that every participant in the market must grasp.

At The Money (ATM): When an option's strike price aligns closely with the current market price of the underlying asset, it is referred to as "at the money." In essence, this situation suggests that the option's strike price and market prices are virtually on par. At-the-money options are like a balance point, as they present no immediate intrinsic value, and the option holder has the potential forneither profit nor loss unless the underlying asset's market price fluctuates. Theyare akin to a financial crossroads, waiting for the market to take a decisive turn.

32

In The Money (ITM): On the other hand, when an option's strike price is advantageous compared to the current market price of the underlying asset, it isconsidered "in the money." In-the-money options, be they call options (for purchasing the asset) or put options (for selling the asset), possess intrinsic value. They enable the option holder to profit through immediate execution, as the option's terms are more favorable than current market conditions. In-the- money options are akin to discovering a treasure chest with contents ready to be claimed.

Out of the Money (OTM): Conversely, options that are deemed "out of the money" when their strike prices are less favorable than the current market priceof the underlying asset. These options lack intrinsic value, and their execution wouldn't be economically advantageous at the present moment. Out-of-the-moneyoptions are a reminder of unrealized potential, akin to a missed opportunity.

However, they are full of utility, as they may hold the allure of future potential if themarket conditions shift.

Note: Understanding the nuances of at the money, in the money, and out of themoney is not merely an academic exercise; it is a fundamental skill for options traders and investors. These distinctions serve as compass points, building decision-making in the complex realm of options trading, helping participants assess risk, potential reward, and the optimal strategies to navigate the dynamic landscape of financial markets.

Elements of the Options Chain:

· **Definition**: An option chain is a table or graphical representation that lists allavailable options contracts for a specific underlying asset. It typically includes the following information for each option contract:

· **Strike Price:** The price at which the option holder has the right to buy (forcall options) or sell (for put options) the underlying asset.

· **Expiration Date:** The date on which the option contract expires, at whichpoint the options become void if not exercised.

· **Type**: Indicates whether the option is a call option (which provides the holderwith the right to buy the underlying asset) or a put option (which gives the holder the right to sell the underlying asset).

· **Bid and Ask Prices:** The current highest price a buyer is willing to pay (bid)and the lowest price a seller is willing to accept (ask) for the option contract.

· **Last Price:** The price at which the most recent trade of the option contractoccurred.

· **Volume:** The total number of contracts traded for that specific option duringthe trading session.

· **Open Interest:** The total number of outstanding contracts for that specificoption.

Key Features and Uses of Option Chains:

1.   **Price Discovery:** Option chains allow traders and investors to see the prices at which options are currently trading. The bid and ask prices provideinsights into the market's assessment of the options' value.

2.   **Risk Management:** Traders can use the option chains to select options withstrike prices and expiration dates that align with their risk tolerance and trading strategies. Different options provide varying degrees of risk and potential reward.

3.   **Expiration Date Selection:** Traders can use option chains to choose option contracts with expiration dates that match their investment horizon or outlook forthe underlying asset.

4.   **Market Sentiment:** The open interest data in an option chain can indicate market sentiment. High open interest on a specific option may suggest significanttrader interest in that contract.

Note: Option chains are widely available through financial platforms, brokeragewebsites, and trading terminals. They are valuable tools for traders and investors who engage in options trading or seek a better understanding of the available options for a specific asset. It's important to note that option chains can vary in format and presentation depending on the trading platform or data provider.

Gamma	Delta	Open Int	% Change	Last	Ask	Bid	Strike	Bid	Ask	Last	% Change	Open Int	Delta
V) 100						# Calls	1 D	Puts %					
0.0075	0.0103	1,730		0.02		0.02	446	8.55		9.10		7	-0.9897
0.0118	0.0165	1,655		0.04		0.04	445	7.55		8.05		15	-0.9835
0.0194	0.0290	1,981		0.07		0.07	444	6.56		8.57	+0.59%	--	-0.9710
0.0318	0.0528	1,990		0.13		0.12	443	5.63		6.75		30	-0.9472
0.0491	0.0937	3,246		0.21		0.21	442	4.76		4.90		61	-0.9063
0.0691	0.1554	2,620	+5.88%	0.36		0.35	441	3.97		4.08		113	-0.8446
0.0880	0.2374	5,290	+12.00%	0.56		0.56	440	3.20		3.26		1,374	-0.7626
0.1022	0.3356	2,242	+17.57%	0.87		0.85	439	2.51		2.57		927	-0.6644
0.1092	0.4432	3,132	+28.28%	1.27		1.25	438	1.93		1.94		3,196	-0.5568
0.1079	0.5526	6,159	+32.58%	1.75		1.75	437	1.43		1.44		3,060	-0.4474
							SPY: 436.32 +1.78 +0.41%						
0.0990	0.6553	3,444	+35.06%	2.35		2.34	436	1.03		1.02		2,708	-0.3447
0.0848	0.7446	2,307	+37.10%	3.03		3.03	435	0.73		0.73		4,358	-0.2554
0.0685	0.8167	2,167	+34.63%	3.81		3.81	434	0.51		0.52		2,854	-0.1833
0.0528	0.8711	1,693	+37.43%	4.70		4.61	433	0.35		0.35		4,600	-0.1289
0.0394	0.9099	3,090	+37.62%	5.56		5.52	432	0.24		0.25		6,201	-0.0901
0.0291	0.9365	2,936	+33.40%	6.39		6.44	431	0.17		0.18		4,618	-0.0635
0.0215	0.9541	4,201	+28.52%	7.30		7.39	430	0.12		0.13		5,922	-0.0459
0.0162	0.9655	1,451	+23.81%	7.80		8.33	429	0.09		0.10		4,142	-0.0345
0.0125	0.9730	2,353	+22.42%	9.01		9.33	428	0.07		0.08		3,829	-0.0270
0.0099	0.9781	1,314	+24.55%	10.30		10.32	427	0.05		0.05		1,670	-0.0219

SRZ Explained

The SRZ (Support and Resistance Zones) is a strategy based on ranges of institutional interest. Support and resistance are not merely lines but zones from the candle wick to the open or close of the candle body. Two types of support andresistance zones are macro (higher timeframes) and micro (lower timeframes).

These zones are of extreme importance since they signify levels where the price reversed, indicating to traders these prices are where the institutions have shownthe most interest. Many traders try to predict the assets' next move, and this is where traders get in trouble. Rather than trying to predict, by using these levels, traders can follow the institutions, making the chances for a profitable trade muchhigher. In conjunction with the zones, using the Dynamic Flow Indicator gives traders added confirmation that the support and resistance price levels are respected.

The image below shows the significance that support and resistance zones haveand the trading opportunities that await.

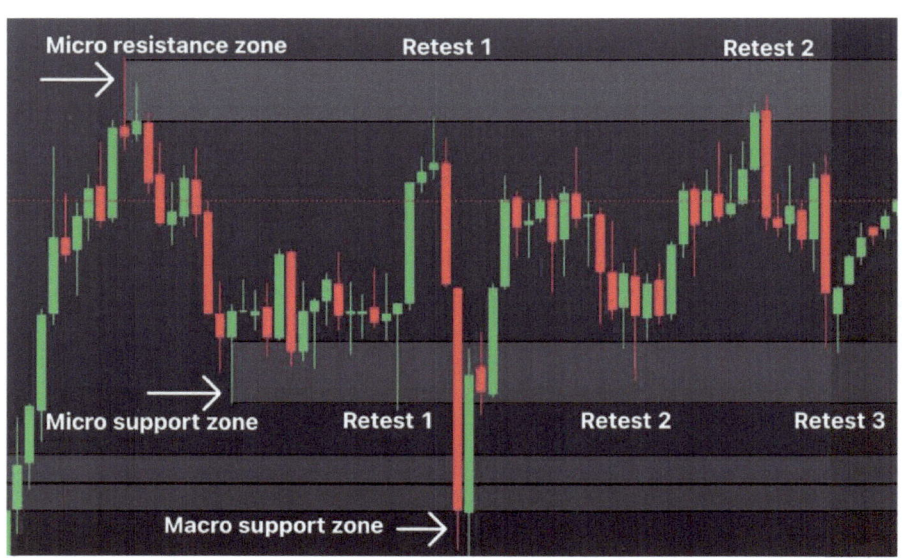

Chart Setup

Setting up the chart is quite simple. The same setup applies to scalping, intradaytrading, or swing trading.

Step 1: Macro Support and Resistance Zones

The macro and micro zones will vary with different timeframes depending on your trading style. In this example, we will use the five-minute timeframe to enter trades.Therefore, we are using the one-hour timeframe for macro zones. We start with fourzones (two above and two below the current price) to keep the charts clean. We're looking for at least three touchpoints close to the same price when determining where to set the zones.

One-Hour Support Zone

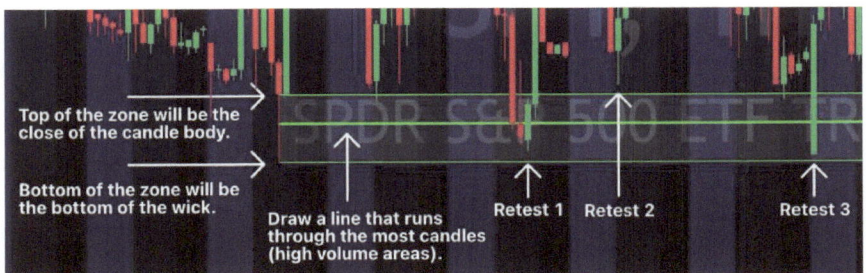

One-Hour Resistance zone

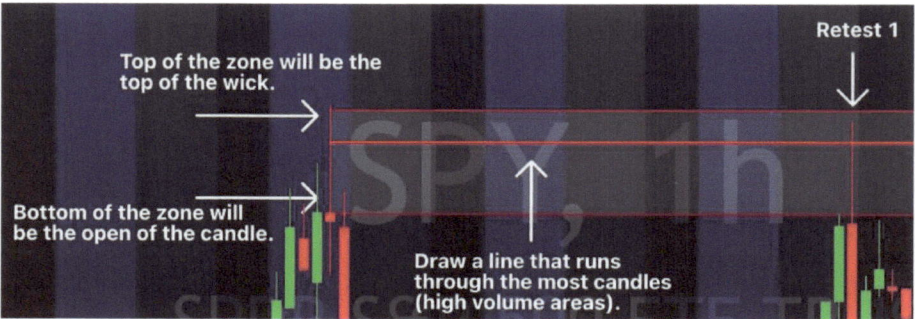

Step 2: Pre-market high and low

Pre-market highs and lows can play a significant role during the trading session. As shown in this example, we see two rejection points from pre-market price reversals.

Step 3: Micro Support and Resistance Zones

Due to the high volatility, it's recommended not to place any trades in the first hourof the market opening. During the first hour, is when reversal zones are marked.

Below are two reversal points; these zones can be beneficial during the trading session, as there were quick scalping opportunities. Smaller timeframes are wheremicro zones are determined.

Entry Signals

Trade Entries: The primary things to watch when entering a trade are the support and resistance zones. When the price approaches a zone, traders will use the Dynamic Flow Indicator for confirmation, which may indicate a trend reversal.

Note: The strategy is the same regardless of the trading style—however, the timeframes change. Below are examples of timeframes for scalping, intraday, and swing trading.

Scalp - macro zones/one-hour, micro zones/one-minute to five-minute.

Intraday - macro zones/one-hour to four-hour, micro zones/15-minute to 30-minute.

Swing - macro zones/four-hour to daily, micro zones/1-hour to four-hour.

Dynamic Flow Indicator Long Signals:

Ascending RSI (green line means the RSI has become bullish).
Light wave cuts into the dark wave.

VWAP is above the zero line.

Money flow is ascending and/or is in the green.

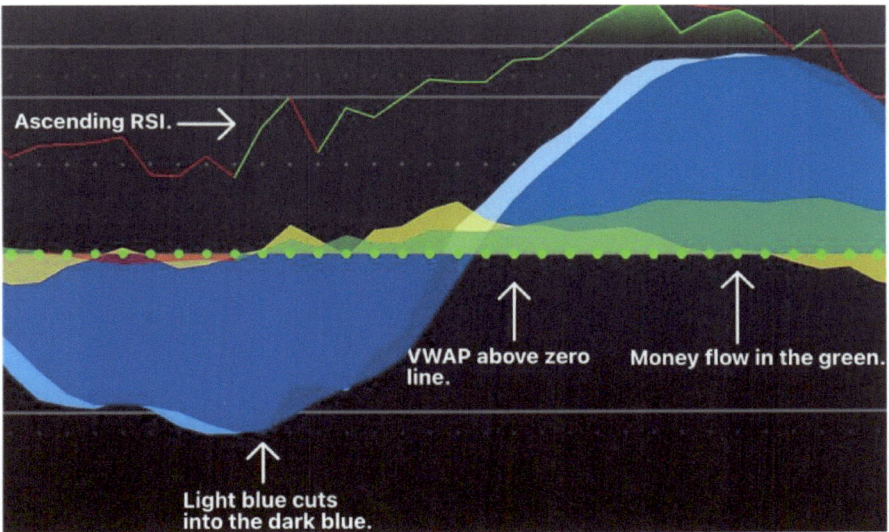

Dynamic Flow Indicator Short Signals:

Descending RSI (red line means the RSI has become bearish). Light wave cuts into the dark wave.

VWAP is below the zero line.

Money flow is descending and/or is in the red.

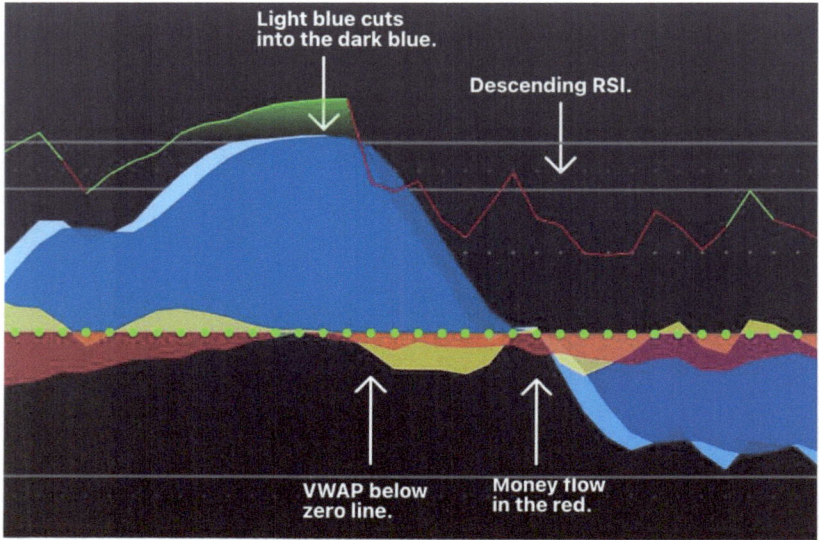

Combining the SRZ and Dynamic Flow Indicator:

As shown in the image below, using the SRZ and DFI is a powerful combination whenspotting a price reversal and finding entry points.

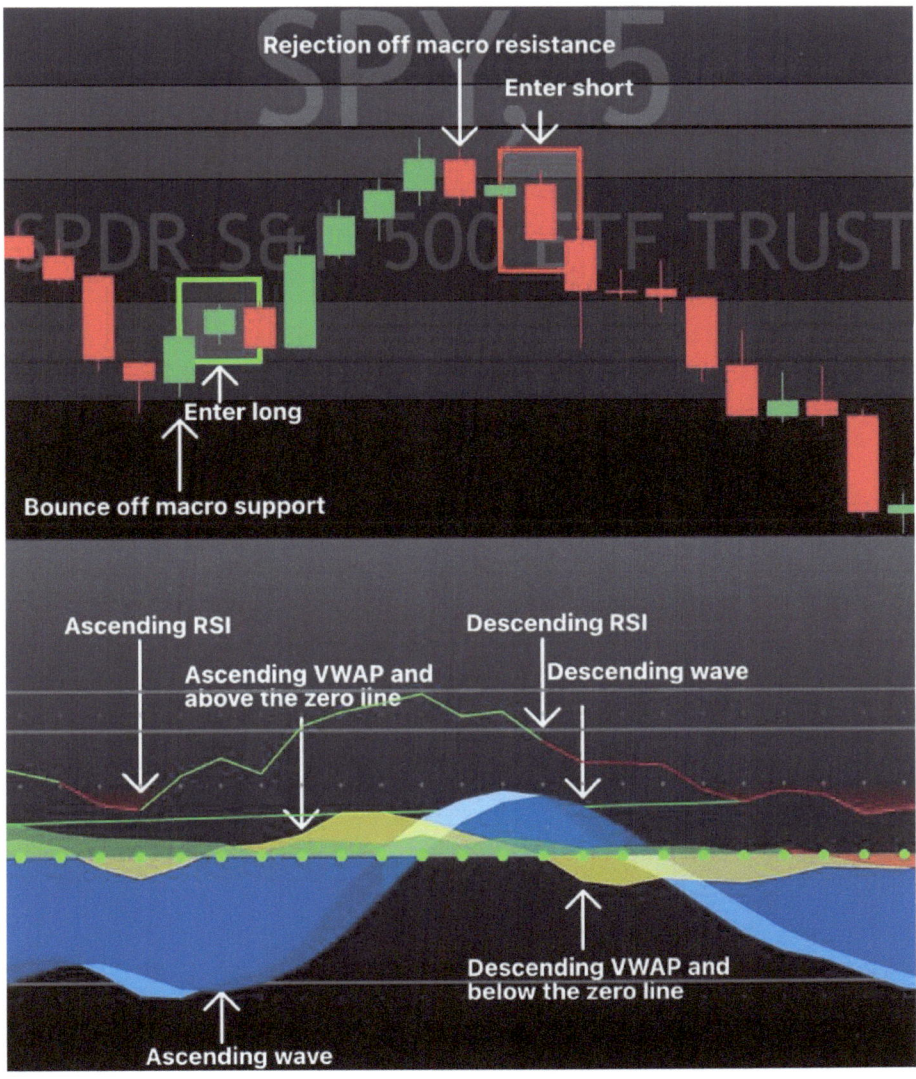

Final Message

The stock market unfolds in finance as a captivating and ever-evolving narrative of human ambition, innovation, and resilience. It is a realm where risk and reward dance in perpetual tandem, the past informs the present, and the future is an unwritten page awaiting the ink of opportunity. It is crucial to recognize that this journey is far from over. The stock market is not just a reflection of our economic aspirations; it is a testament to our capacity to adapt, learn, and, above all, grow.

As we step away from these pages, armed with knowledge and insight, let us remember that the stock market, at its core, is a story of progress shaped by countless minds and hands that have come before us and those that will follow. With this understanding, we can navigate this ever-shifting landscape with wisdom,year after year, trade after trade. The final lesson is that the stock market is not solely a realm of profit and loss but a classroom of life's most profound lessons. It teaches patience, resilience, and adaptability. It reminds us that, in the end, success is not solely measured by wealth but by the knowledge we gain, the experiences we accumulate, and the growth we achieve. In closing, the book of thestock market remains open, ready for the next generation of investors, dreamers, and innovators to pen their own stories, create their strategies, and embark on theirfinancial journeys. With its infinite potential and boundless opportunities, the stockmarket is a living, breathing testament to the relentless spirit of human endeavor.

Disclaimer

TradexPro, LLC and/or its owners, and all affiliated parties and team members are not registered as Financial Advisors and hold no qualifications to offer financial advice. All content by TradxPro, LLC and/or its owners and all affiliates or team members is for educational purposes only and should not be taken as financial advice. TradexPro, LLC is not liable for any loss or damages. No strategy is a hundred percent profitable, and therefore, traders should always use proper risk management. You must know the risks and accept full responsibility when investingin the financial markets. Therefore, assess your financial situation and consider if the trading risk is suitable.

www.ingramcontent.com/pod-product-compliance
Lightning Source LLC
Chambersburg PA
CBHW050836290526
45792CB00001B/411